Quiz: 117565

RL
6.4
pts.
1.0

Natural Disasters

Volcanoes

Louise Park

A⁺

Smart Apple Media

This edition first published in 2008 in the United States of America by Smart Apple Media.

Smart Apple Media
2140 Howard Drive West
North Mankato, Minnesota 56003

First published in 2007 by
MACMILLAN EDUCATION AUSTRALIA PTY LTD
627 Chapel Street, South Yarra, Australia 3141

Visit our Web site at www.macmillan.com.au or go directly to www.macmillanlibrary.com.au

Associated companies and representatives throughout the world.

Library of Congress Cataloging-in-Publication Data

Park, Louise, 1961-
Volcanoes / by Louise Park.
   p. cm. – (Natural disasters)
   Includes index.
   ISBN 978-1-59920-110-8
   1. Volcanoes–Juvenile literature. 2. Natural disasters–Juvenile literature. I. Title.

   QE521.3.P374 2007
   551.21–dc22

                                                  2007004775

Edited by Sam Munday and Erin Richards
Text and cover design by Ivan Finnegan, iF design
Page layout by Ivan Finnegan, iF design
Photo research by Jes Senbergs
Illustrations by Andy Craig and Nives Porcellato, p. 9
Maps by designscope, pp. 6, 10, 12 (top and bottom), 16, 24

Printed in U.S.

Acknowledgements
The author and the publisher are grateful to the following for permission to reproduce copyright material:
Front cover photograph: molten lava flowing from a Hawaiian volcano, courtesy of Bernhard Edmaier /Science Photo Library.

Background textures courtesy of Ivan Finnegan, iF design.

AFP Photo/Tarko Sudlarno /AAP Image, p. 22; Dimas Ardian /Getty Images, p. 5; AusAid/Dominic Morice , p. 21; AusAid/Rocky Roe, p. 14 (left); Yann Arthus-Bertrand/Corbis, p. 15 (top);Bernhard Edmaier/Science Photo Library, pp. 1, 15 (bottom), 17; Simon Fraser/Mauna Loa Observatory/Science Photo Library, pp. 19, 27; Peter Menzell/Science Photo Library, p. 18; NASA, p. 6; NASA/Science Photo Library, p. 16; NGDS, p. 13; Jos van Noord/MSF, p. 23; Chuck Pefley/Alamy, p. 28; Popperfoto/Alamy, pp.25, 24; Dr Morley Read/Science Photo Library, pp. 4, 29; Reuters/Picture Media, p. 8; Joseph Baylor Roberts/Getty Images, p. 14 (right); Ronaldo Schemidt/Getty Images, p. 20; Michael T. Sedam /Corbis, p. 11; URI News Bureau, p. 7; Zephyr /Science Photo Library, p. 26.

While every care has been taken to trace and acknowledge copyright, the publisher tenders their apologies for any accidental infringement where copyright has proved untraceable. Where the attempt has been unsuccessful, the publisher welcomes information that would redress the situation.

Contents

Natural disasters 4

Volcanoes 5

Disaster file Tambora, Indonesia 6

Inside Earth 8

Where volcanoes form 10

Disaster file The Ring of Fire 12

Volcano shapes 14

Disaster file Mauna Loa, Hawaii 16

Magma and lava 18

When a volcano erupts 20

Disaster file Mount Pelée, Martinique 24

Studying volcanoes 26

Disaster relief 28

Disaster files at a glance 30

Glossary 31

Index 32

GLOSSARY WORDS
When a word is printed in **bold**, you can look up its meaning in the glossary on page 31.

Natural disasters

Natural disasters are events that occur naturally. They are not caused by human action. They can happen all over the world at any time. When natural disasters occur in populated areas, they can result in death, injury, and damage to property.

Types of natural disasters

There are many types of natural disasters, such as tornadoes, wildfires, droughts, and earthquakes. Each type occurs for very different reasons and affects the Earth in different ways. Although they are different, they all create chaos and bring **devastation** and destruction with them wherever they strike.

Volcanic eruptions in populated areas can be devastating.

Volcanoes

Volcanic eruptions shake the surface of our planet every year. Most of these occur in places where not many people live, but occasionally a volcano erupts in a populated area.

What is a volcano?

A volcano is a place on Earth's surface where **molten** rock and other **debris** erupt through Earth's **crust**. Some volcanoes are nothing more than cracks in Earth's crust. Others are domes, shields, or mountain-like structures.

Lava leaks from openings like this in Earth's crust.

DID YOU KNOW?
Volcanoes are named after the Roman god, Vulcan. Vulcan was the Roman god of fire.

Why do we have volcanoes?

Volcanic eruptions are a natural way for Earth to cool off and release pressure. Deep inside Earth, intense heat and pressure cause rock to melt. This molten rock rises and pushes its way to the surface, creating a volcanic eruption. When **magma** erupts out of a volcano like this, it is called **lava**.

DISASTER FILE
Tambora, Indonesia

WHAT	The greatest volcanic eruption in recorded history
WHERE	The Indonesian island of Sumbawa
WHEN	April 5–10, 1815
EXPLOSIVITY INDEX	7

Tambora had been silent for over 5,000 years before erupting in 1815. Small eruptions began in 1812 and continued until the first big eruption on April 5, 1815. This eruption was heard over 620 miles (1,000 km) away. The second deadly series of explosions took place five days later. These explosions created columns of volcanic material that stretched 25 miles (40 km) into the sky. When these columns collapsed, enormous amounts of deadly ash, rock, and **pumice** spread across the island, killing everything in their path.

Tambora, as seen from space, dominates the island of Sumbawa.

Why did it happen?

Scientists believe that ocean water began seeping into cracks and fissures within the volcano. When the ocean water mixed with magma, an enormous amount of pressure built up inside the volcano. When the pressure became too great, the volcano erupted and blew apart.

Counting the cost

The massive output of hot ash and rock almost wiped out the entire population of Tambora. When the flows reached the sea, they produced tsunamis that devastated neighboring islands. The ash destroyed villages, farmland, crops, and soil. The estimated death toll was 92,000. Around 10,000 people were killed directly by bomb impacts and **pyroclastic flows.** The major cause of death was starvation and disease as a result of these large ash flows.

Think about it

This eruption changed weather patterns around the world. So much volcanic ash was unleashed into the atmosphere that the following year became known as the "Year Without a Summer." Average global temperatures decreased by about 0.5°F (0.3°C) and caused significant agricultural problems all around the world.

Scientists have unearthed remains from the lost civilization of Tambora, which was buried under tons of hot ash and rock.

Inside Earth

Inside Earth there are three main layers. They are the crust, the **mantle**, and the **core**.

The crust

The outermost surface layer of Earth is called the crust. The crust is made of cold rock, only about 43 miles (70 km) thick, and is quite brittle. It is here that cracks and fissures appear and molten rock can leak out to form a volcano.

The mantle

The mantle is the thickest of the three layers. It starts just below the crust and extends to the core of Earth. The mantle is made of hot rock. Some parts are so hot that the rock has melted. This thick, molten substance is called magma. It is magma that pushes its way to the surface, causing a volcano to erupt.

Magma bursts out of a fissure in Earth's crust, forming a volcano.

The core

Beneath the mantle is Earth's core. It has two layers:

- the outer core

- the inner core

The core is made of metal. The outer core contains iron that is so hot that it is in liquid form. The inner core is even hotter yet it seems solid. This is because the pressure from all the other layers pushes the inner core into a tight lump that cannot move anywhere. This part of Earth experiences great pressure. Its temperature can range from 6,300 to 9,000°F (3,500 to 5,000°C).

Earth's crust is the thinnest layer and the most brittle.

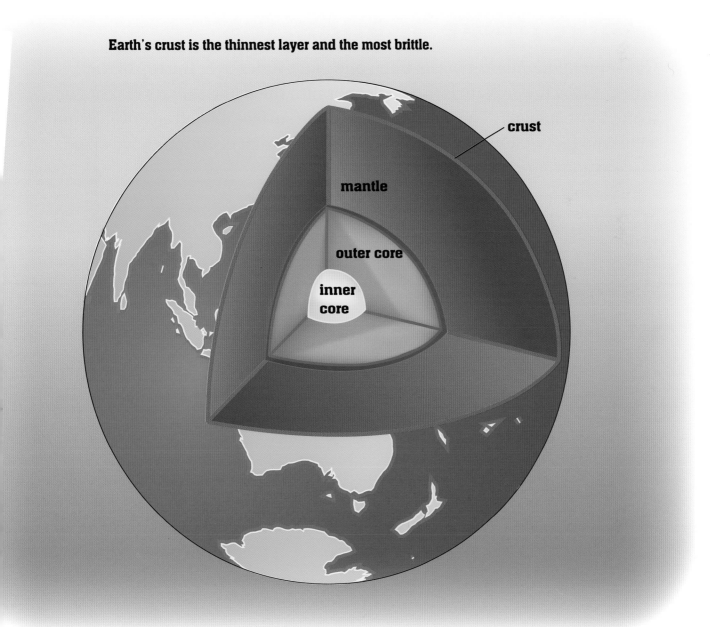

Where volcanoes form

Most volcanoes occur on the edges or boundaries of the **tectonic plates** that make up Earth's crust. Sometimes they can form in the middle of these plates, in areas known as hotspots. There are seven major tectonic plates. They float on the magma that flows through the mantle. As the magma flows underneath them, it pushes the plates and causes them to bump and rub together at their boundaries.

Convergent boundaries

Convergent boundaries occur when one plate slides over the top of the other. As the lower plate is forced deeper into the mantle, parts of it begin to melt into magma. This magma rises to the surface and often erupts from a volcano in a violent way. Most of the world's worst eruptions have taken place at convergent boundaries.

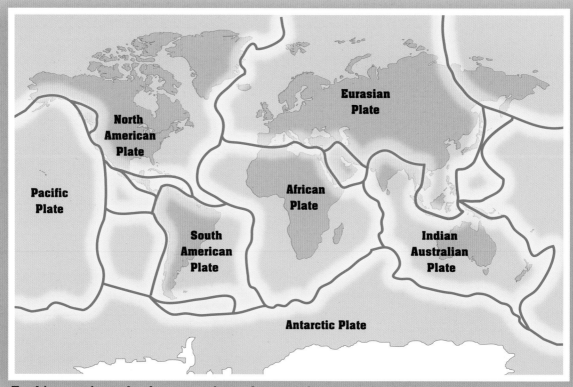

Earth's crust is made of seven major and many minor tectonic plates.

Divergent boundaries

Divergent boundaries occur when two plates move away from each other. As they move away, magma from the mantle swells up into the crack and cools. This creates more crust in the ocean floor. As the plates move further apart, the ocean floor expands. This is known as sea-floor spreading. Divergent eruptions are less violent, with lava coming out in a smooth, flowing manner.

Hotspots

Hotspots are areas where magma continuously breaks through a tectonic plate. These hotspots act like a pipeline for magma. Magma from deep within the mantle pushes its way up to Earth's surface. When a plate is over one of these hotspots, the magma pushes through the plate to the surface. When this happens, volcanic islands are formed. After a period of millions of years, the island moves beyond the hotspot, cutting off the source of magma, and a new island begins to form. The Hawaiian Islands are the most famous example of volcanic islands formed from hotspots.

DID YOU KNOW?
About 500 million people live close to active volcanoes. On the island of Hawaii, people even live on active volcanoes. These volcanoes are closely monitored by scientists so that risk from volcanic hazards can be reduced.

The Hawaiian Islands were formed over a hotspot.

DISASTER FILE
The Ring of Fire

WHAT	A zone of frequent earthquakes and volcanic activity
WHERE	An arc encircling the basin of the Pacific Ocean

The Ring of Fire is an arc that contains over 75 percent of the world's active and **dormant** volcanoes. It is located at the borders of the Pacific Plate and other tectonic plates. The Ring of Fire is a direct result of tectonic plates in action. Around the Ring of Fire, the Pacific Plate is colliding with and sliding underneath other plates. This creates a number of **subduction zones**. There is an enormous amount of energy created by these plates. Energy released at subduction zones is usually much greater than energy released in other plate tectonics. These zones easily melt rock into magma, which then creates volcanoes.

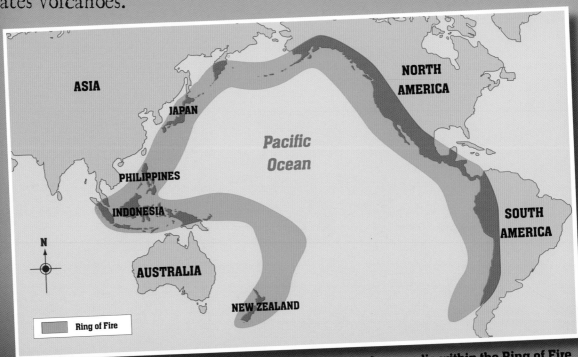

Many of the world's active volcanoes lie within the Ring of Fire.

Eruptions in the Ring of Fire

There is a lot of activity in the Ring of Fire due to the large number of active volcanoes within it. The type of eruptions and the damage produced varies greatly. Mount St. Helens is the most destructive volcano in the history of the United States. It sits in the Ring of Fire.

After being dormant for 123 years, Mount St. Helens erupted on May 18, 1980. During its eruption, ash, steam, and gas blasted out with incredible force. The northern slope of Mount St. Helens collapsed under the pressure. Ice, snow, and water mixed with lava to create mudflows. Fifty-seven people were killed and the damage to land and wildlife was significant.

The eruption of Mount St. Helens reduced its height by 1,312 feet (400 m).

Volcano shapes

The shape of a volcano takes time to form. Each eruption, no matter how small, contributes to its growth and shape. There are three main types of volcanoes and each has its own shape. These are stratovolcanoes, shield volcanoes, and scoria or cinder cone volcanoes.

Stratovolcanoes

Stratovolcanoes are the most familiar type of volcanoes and they have a history of violent and destructive eruptions. They are steep and cone-shaped and can take tens to hundreds of thousands of years to form. Stratovolcanoes mostly occur at convergent boundaries and tend to erupt hundreds of years apart.

Shield volcanoes

Shield volcanoes have wide, gentle slopes. The lava that erupts from these volcanoes flows easily across the ground. It spreads over a wide surface area, forming a shield-shaped dome. The largest volcanoes on Earth are shield volcanoes. These volcanoes occur at divergent boundaries and over hotspots. Many shield volcanoes erupt every few years.

Shield volcanoes are wide with gentle slopes.

Stratovolcanoes are conical in shape.

Scoria or cinder cone volcanoes

Cinder cones have steep slopes that lead to a very wide opening. They are the most common type of volcano. Cinder cones vary in size, with some reaching 1,000 feet (300 m) in height. Many scoria or cinder cone volcanoes erupt only once.

Calderas and volcanic domes

Sometimes volcanic activity can produce calderas and volcanic domes. Calderas are large circular basins that sit at the top of a volcano. Calderas are created when magma is withdrawn from underground magma pools. This causes the ground and rock to collapse. Often these basins fill up with water to create lakes.

Volcanic domes occur when magma cools quickly and does not flow out. The magma cools around the top of the volcano like a domed plug. These dome shapes tend to be steep at the sides.

Cinder cones are known for their wide openings.

Crater Lake is a caldera, formed when an ancient volcano collapsed.

DISASTER FILE
Mauna Loa, Hawaii

WHAT	The largest volcano in the world
WHERE	Hawaii, U.S.
WHEN	First documented eruption was in 1843, most recent eruption was April 1984

EXPLOSIVITY INDEX	0

Mauna Loa takes up half the island of Hawaii. It rises a massive 2.5 miles (4 km) above sea level and descends another 3 miles (5 km) to the sea floor. Below the sea floor, it is believed to extend another 5 miles (8 km.) This makes Mauna Loa the largest volcano in the world, with its **summit** around 10.5 miles (17 km) from its base. It is a shield volcano formed from a hotspot.

Why does Mauna Loa exist?

Mauna Loa is part of a chain of volcanoes that were formed as they passed over a hotspot. This chain is now known as the Hawaiian Islands. After more than one million years of eruptions and lava oozing and cooling, these shield volcanoes became big enough to be islands. Mauna Loa is the biggest and most active of these.

Mauna Loa is a shield volcano formed from a hotspot.

Counting the cost

Mauna Loa is one of the most active volcanoes on Earth. It has erupted more than 30 times since 1843. Mauna Loa is considered a "non-explosive" volcano. Eruptions produce lava flows but very little **tephra** is ejected. Loss of life due to eruptions has not happened since the end of the last century. Damage to property and land, however, does continue to take place. Mauna Loa's eruptions sometimes last for weeks, allowing lava flows to travel over a lot of land and even reach the sea. The most recent eruption was on April 24, 1984. The eruption lasted three weeks with lava pouring out like a river. Destruction by lava flows destroyed land and **vegetation.**

DID YOU KNOW?
Mauna Loa means "long mount" in Hawaiian.

Trees in the path of the lava flows are burned and buried under molten rock.

Magma and lava

The shape of the volcano and how it behaves depends on the magma it produces. Different mixtures of magma produce different types of lava.

Magma

Magma is made of melted rocks, which are made of all sorts of different minerals. These minerals all melt at different temperatures. Rocks also contain a lot of dissolved gases. When these gases expand, they form small gas bubbles in the magma.

When magma is filled with lots of these tiny gas bubbles, it pushes out and escapes. This process is similar to shaking a soft drink bottle. When the bottle is shaken, the gas pushes up and tries to escape. The result is an eruption of gas and liquid. Similarly, when a volcano erupts, the bubbles escape and push magma out with them. The type of lava produced depends on the minerals and gases in the magma.

Magma erupts from a volcano like a shaken soft drink escaping from a bottle.

DID YOU KNOW?
The hottest lava occurs in the volcanoes of the Hawaiian Islands. Lava here can reach temperatures between 2,100 and 2,150°F (1,150 and 1,175°C.)

Lava

Magma that reaches Earth's surface is called lava. Generally there are three types of lava: basaltic, rhyolitic, and andesite.

Basaltic lava

Basaltic lava cools to form basalt rock, which is hard and black. The lava flows quickly and easily and is the most common form of lava. Basaltic lava fountains can be hundreds of feet tall.

Rhyolitic lava

Rhyolitic lava cools to form rhyolite rock, which is a light-colored rock. Rhyolitic lava is the least common form of lava. This lava struggles to flow freely and generally cools and hardens quickly.

Andesite lava

Andesite lava cools to form andesite rock, which is a greyish-black rock. Andesite lava contains more dissolved gases than other lava types. It also moves quickly and freely. Andesite lava makes enormous, explosive eruptions and thick lava flows and surges. Andesite lava commonly erupts from stratovolcanoes.

Think about it

Iceland is famous for the smallest and largest lava flows in history. The smallest was 35.3 cubic yards ($27 m^3$) in 1977. The largest was 3 cubic miles ($12.3 km^3$) in 1783.

This basaltic lava, erupted from Kilauea, Hawaii, flowed more than 6 miles (10 km) before reaching the sea on the Hawaiian coast.

When a volcano erupts

When a volcano erupts, magma bursts out and pours down its sides. Gas, steam, and tephra often shoot into the sky as well. Sometimes the eruption can be so loud it sounds like an explosion. As magma rises up from the mantle, it cools and some of it becomes solid. These solid pieces get blasted out in the eruption.

Steam can also be blown into the air. When there is a lot of steam, it can cause a rainstorm. Sometimes the steam mixes with ash to make a thick mud. Volcanic eruptions vary a great deal. Some volcanoes explode violently causing a lot of damage and destruction. Others seep out lava so slowly that you can safely walk around it.

Volcanic eruptions can blow enormous amounts of steam into the air.

Lava flows

Lava can erupt in both explosive and non-explosive ways. Lava flows destroy everything in their path, but most flows move slowly enough for people to move out of their way. The speed at which lava moves depends mainly on the steepness of the ground and the type of lava it is.

Volcanic ash

Volcanic ash is made of volcanic rock and glass fragments. It is solid and is created during explosive eruptions. In a large eruption, ash can fly out in enormous columns. It can cover large areas, which can make it a greater hazard than lava. In 1951, ash flows killed nearly 3,000 people when Lamington erupted in Papua New Guinea.

Columns of volcanic ash can rise many miles into the air.

Pyroclastic flows

Pyroclastic flows are mixtures of hot tephra and gases that move at high speeds. They generally flow from stratovolcanoes. Most pyroclastic flows move along the ground but create clouds of ash that rise above the ground. Pyroclastic flows will destroy nearly everything in their path. They can contain rock fragments the size of boulders that can hurtle down the slopes at incredible speeds. These flows can travel up to 656 feet (200 m) per second and the heat of the flow can reach over 930°F (500°C). Pyroclastic flows can cause the greatest devastation of any type of eruption.

Pyroclastic flows are sometimes known as burning clouds.

Think about it

Many pyroclastic flows can come from one volcano. When Mount Pinatubo had a massive eruption in 1991, it triggered flows that continued for more than two years.

Mud and debris flows

Mud and debris that flow down the sides of a volcano are another serious hazard. Debris flows often form when part of a volcano collapses. If the collapse is large enough, flows can travel great distances and bury everything in their way.

Measuring eruptions

The Volcanic Explosivity Index was developed in 1982. It is a scale that measures the explosiveness of eruptions. The scale looks at the volume of tephra that is ejected from the volcano and the height of the eruption clouds.

DID YOU KNOW?
When Mount St. Helens erupted in 1980, a great deal of rock and debris was thrown from the mountain. This rock and debris traveled as fast as 250 miles (400 km) an hour.

More than 23,000 people were killed from mud and debris flows when Nevado del Ruiz erupted on November 13, 1985.

DISASTER FILE
Mount Pelée, Martinique

WHAT	The worst volcanic disaster of the 1900s
WHERE	Martinique in the West Indies
WHEN	The main eruption was on May 8, 1902
EXPLOSIVITY INDEX	4

A pyroclastic flow swept toward the city of
Saint Pierre, killing everything in its path.

Mount Pelée is an active stratovolcano. On April 25, 1902, it began erupting and slowly built into a massive eruption that occurred on May 8.

During the build-up to the huge eruption, many people moved into the city from the countryside in hopes of finding safety. On the morning of May 8, the upper mountainside tore apart and a dense pyroclastic flow shot out with great force. This was followed directly by a vertical pyroclastic cloud that mushroomed above the mountain and covered the sky around it. The eruption destroyed the city of Saint Pierre in minutes.

Why did it happen?

Mount Pelée is one of a number of volcanoes in the 435 mile (700 km) long Lesser Antilles island arc. This arc was formed as a result of the oceanic crust of the South American Plate subducting under the oceanic crust of the small Caribbean Plate. Scientists are not really sure why Mount Pelée erupted, but the volcano is studied very closely. It is an excellent example of how deadly pyroclastic flows from stratovolcanoes can be.

Counting the cost

The pyroclastic cloud rushed down the mountain at speeds of up to 416 miles (670 km) an hour. In less than a minute, it had reached the city of Saint Pierre, burning everything it came into contact with. The cloud of steam, dust, and volcanic ash destroyed the city. Sources report that there were only two survivors: a man locked underground in a prison and another who lived on the outskirts of the city.

The city of Saint Pierre was completely destroyed.

Think about it

The Lesser Antilles are a chain of volcanic islands. There are currently 16 volcanoes there and 13 of them are stratovolcanoes.

Studying volcanoes

Volcanologists are scientists who study volcanoes. They use clues from the volcano itself and special instruments to predict eruptions.

Before an eruption

Before an eruption, magma moves closer to the surface of a volcano. When it does, it releases gases. Volcanologists can study these gases, as well as how the magma is moving, to make predictions about eruptions. Studying magma as it rises closer to the surface helps scientists with their predictions. When magma moves, it can cause small earthquakes which are picked up by tools such as seismographs.

Seismographs

Seismographs pick up the vibrations coming from an earthquake and record them as a wavy line. When volcanoes are preparing to erupt, there is an increase in **seismic activity**. This is picked up by seismographs and alerts volcanologists to what is happening.

Scientists use seismographs to measure movement and vibrations inside Earth.

Gas emissions and ground swelling

Scientists can examine the gases given off by rising magma for sulfur dioxide levels. Increasing amounts of sulfur dioxide indicate an increase in the amount of magma reaching the surface.

As magma rises to the surface, the shape of the volcano can sometimes change as well. Volcanologists can measure the angle of the slope and record any changes. Swelling indicates a buildup of magma near the surface. Such a change in the gas emitted and swelling indicates that an eruption is imminent.

Even with the best knowledge and equipment, it is still difficult to know exactly when an eruption will happen. It is also difficult to know how big that eruption might be.

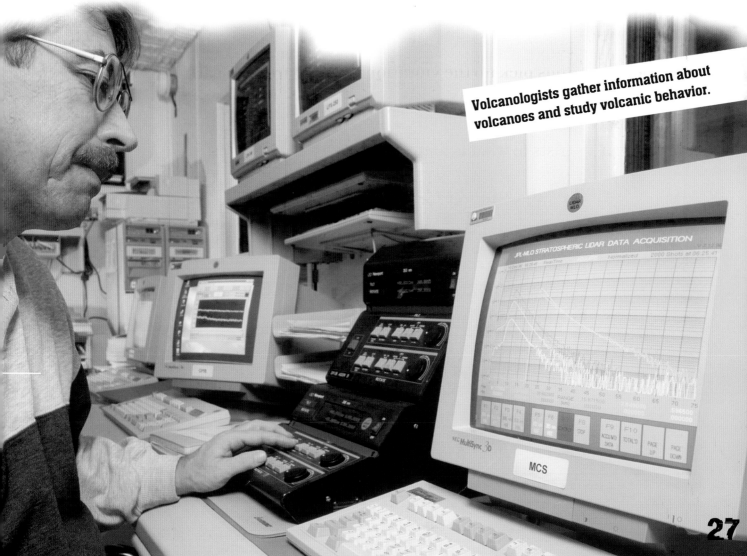

Volcanologists gather information about volcanoes and study volcanic behavior.

Disaster relief

When a volcano has finished erupting, there is much to be done. The first step is to rescue any survivors. People can be caught under debris or left stranded and homeless. Areas are set up where relief can be provided to victims. People may need more than medical attention. They frequently need dry clothing, shelter, food, and fresh water as well.

Rebuilding

After relief efforts have been established, workers can assess the damage and begin cleaning up. Dangerously damaged structures need to be demolished. Finally, rebuilding begins. Often people have to start all over again. The costs of rebuilding communities can be massive. This can place strain on the economy of the country and on its government. Sometimes, extensive damage attracts aid from other countries that wish to help.

More than one million people live in the shadow of Mount Rainer, an active stratovolcano in the U.S.

The benefits of volcanic activity

Volcanic eruptions can cause damage and destruction, but they also have benefits. Valuable resources such as zinc, uranium, and mercury form within volcanoes. Minerals found in volcanoes enrich the soil, which helps with farming and crops. Volcanoes can create islands and make new mountains. They also allow Earth to release pressure and heat. They can be very destructive, but they are also crucial to Earth and our ongoing environment.

Many people are drawn to the rich, green slopes of a volcano.

DISASTER FILES AT A GLANCE

The four volcanoes profiled in this book are record-breaking for different reasons. This graph shows their volcanic explosivity index and their death tolls.

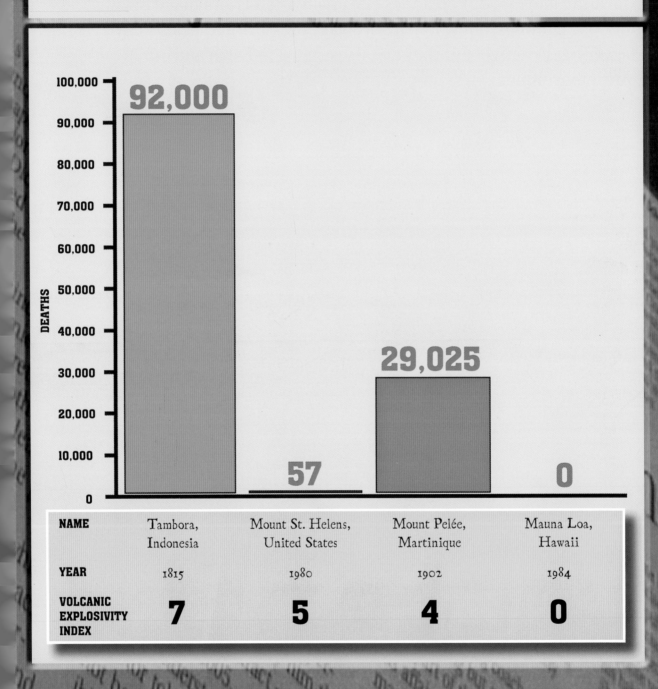

NAME	Tambora, Indonesia	Mount St. Helens, United States	Mount Pelée, Martinique	Mauna Loa, Hawaii
YEAR	1815	1980	1902	1984
VOLCANIC EXPLOSIVITY INDEX	7	5	4	0

DEATHS

92,000

29,025

57

0

Glossary

core the center of Earth

crust the hard surface layer of Earth

debris the remains of things that have been broken or destroyed

devastation severe damage or destruction

dormant asleep or inactive

lava hot, liquid rock that has erupted from a volcano

magma hot, liquid rock under Earth's surface

mantle layer of hot rock beneath Earth's crust

molten made liquid by heat

pumice light and glassy volcanic rock

pyroclastic flows hot mixtures of rock, ash, and gases that move along the ground at high speeds

seismic activity the shaking and vibrations inside Earth

subduction zones areas where one tectonic plate is forced below another

summit the very top of a mountain

tectonic plates large plates of rock that make up Earth's crust

tephra solid material, such as ash and rock, that erupts from a volcano

vegetation the plants of an area

Index

A

aid   28
ash   6-7, 13, 21, 25

C

caldera   15
cinder cone   14, 15
convergent
        boundaries   10, 14
core   8-9
crust   5, 8-9, 11, 25

D

debris   5, 23
divergent boundaries   11,
        14
dormant   12-13

G

gas   18-19, 22, 26-27
ground swelling   27

H

Hawaiian Islands   11, 16
hotspot   10-11, 16

L

lava flow   17, 19, 21
lava types   19

M

magma   12, 15, 18-19,
        20, 26, 27
mantle   8-9, 10, 11, 20
Mauna Loa,
        Hawaii   16-17, 30
measuring   23
minerals   18, 29
Mount Pelée, Martinique
        24-25, 30
Mount St. Helens, United
        States   13, 23
mudflow   13, 23

N

natural disasters,
        types of   4
non-explosive   17, 21

P

pyroclastic flows   7, 22,
        24-25

R

rebuilding   28
relief   28
rescue   28
resources   29
Ring of Fire   12-13

S

scoria volcano   14, 15
seafloor spreading   11
seismograph   26
shield volcano   5, 14, 16
stratovolcano   14, 19, 22,
        24, 25
subduction zone   12, 25

T

Tambora, Indonesia   6-7,
        30
tectonic plates   10-11, 12,
        25
tephra   17, 20, 22-23
tsunami   7

V

volcanic dome   5, 15
Volcanic Explosivity
        Index   6, 16,
        23, 24
volcanologist   26, 27